New York Apartments
Private Views

ts

Jamee Gregory

Design by Charles Davey

Photography by Mick Hales

RIZZOLI
NEW YORK

Contents

Who has not dreamed of a perfect pied-à-terre   9

Stretching one hundred feet along Central Park   17

A spectacular duplex   27

North of the United Nations   37

Perched high above upper Park Avenue,   45

Views from Central Park South   57

A vast collection of modern art   69

Above the 59th Street bridge   79

"Everything about this Fifth Avenue apartment attracted me,"   89

In this midtown apartment   97

A renowned architect decided   105

Superb views of Central Park   113

The owner of this majestic apartment   *121*

Can an apartment change a life?   *129*

On two floors of a limestone townhouse   *135*

High ceilings, a sweeping staircase,   *145*

In this midtown pied-à-terre   *153*

'Twenty-foot ceilings, a forty-foot room …'   *159*

This Gracie Square apartment   *167*

Located in one of Mantattan's premier buildings   *177*

Boasting fine views of the East River   *187*

On a Tribeca Street   *199*

Acknowledgments   *208*

Photo Credits   *208*

NewYorkApartments
Private Views

Who has not dreamed of a perfect pied-à-terre

overlooking Central Park? The owner of this apartment, in a premier 1927 landmark building, can enjoy views high above New York's celebrated Grand Army Plaza and hotel service, like a grown-up Eloise, when she and her husband arrive in New York, several times a year.

A fanciful red Regency lantern, a bright coral ribbon over a Swedish starburst gilt clock, a demi-lune table holding flowers in a vivid jardinière, and a curving Regency bench covered in green moiré, complete this illusion of a garden.

Undeterred by the apartment's initially lackluster state, she trusted the sure hand and expert eye of designer Mario Buatta to heed her only requirement: "Make it English." Working with architect John Murray, then a partner in the firm of Ferguson, Murray and Shamamian, Buatta invigorated the interior by raising the height of the doors and adding huge openings in long walls. They connected the paneled library with the dining room in order to create a natural flow for entertaining. Original crown moldings were restored and recreated, and an artificial fireplace installed.

Buatta transformed a dreary, window-less entrance hall into a virtual English garden. He commissioned the late Robert Jackson to hand paint murals replete with pavilions, urns, trees, and flowers, serving to create the illusion of walking outdoors.

In the library / dining room a drum table, hunting paintings, an English Regency-style sideboard, Georgian wheel-back side chairs, and tortoise shades evoke an English country home. Buatta installed specially made handcrafted mahogany panels.

Taking advantage of this cozy room, the couple often orders dinner for two from the hotel's well-known restaurant, requiring only a small butler's pantry, hidden behind doors in a corner of the room, in place of a kitchen.

BELOW: *Buatta has framed the spectacular views, which can be seen from every window, in simple but effective dressing.*

Employing his characteristic mix of chintz and color, Buatta used striped draperies—to suggest height—in the living room, covered the sofas with blue and cream damask, glazed the walls his signature sunny yellow, and added white woodwork. A flowered Aubusson-style rug anchors the room. Buatta also found ideal antiques, like the japanned green-lacquered Queen Anne secretary, an early eighteenth-century stool, and a Chinese porcelain garden seat. He placed a nineteenth-century mantel, over which he hung an eighteenth-century carved and gilded mirror, adding depth, and hung his client's American Impressionist paintings: "Maine Blossoms" by Edward Willis Redfield and "A Lady Reading" by Richard Edward Miller. Bibelots were chosen and placed on lacquered coffee tables.

Reconfiguring the back hall and bedrooms, Buatta created a small foyer for book cases and cupboards. His-and-her bathrooms are black and white. The jungle-themed guest room has a Regency bed with Chippendale-style canopy. Animal prints cover one wall.

In the main bedroom, dressmaker details, such as tasseled fringes, festooned valances, a ribbon-bordered chaise longue, and a full-skirted dressing table—with candlestick lamps, piped and pleated—exemplify Buatta's style: smart, comfortable, and sumptuous. Buatta's transformation of this blank space demonstrates the advantages of the seldom-practiced "Surprise Me!" school of decorating.

RIGHT: *In the guest bedroom flowing floral chintz envelops a delicately-painted four-poster bed, creating a room-within-a-room. Reading lights with pleated shades-on-arms hang over a quilted headboard, covered with scalloped pillows.*

Stretching one hundred feet along Central Park

this dazzling apartment did not initially appeal to its current owner, but she was soon convinced by her husband. Few apartments boast a forty-foot gallery, and sixty-five hundred square feet on one floor. "He called Bunny Williams, who had already decorated two apartments for me. She immediately knew what to do, having worked in the building before." Williams explained to the couple: "If you can't find the apartment you want, you have to create your own!"

LEFT: *"The gallery was meticulously restored by our own Michelangelo!"*

PRECEDING PAGES: *"The most lived-in room is our red-lacquered library, which is filled with personal mementoes and books."*

ABOVE *and* RIGHT: *The stately living room was filled with comfortable sofas, a piano, family photographs and a favorite dog picture found at the Winter Antiques Show.*

With the help of architect Nasser Nakib, Williams completely transformed the space. The apartment had been redone in the fifties by architect Philip Johnson, who had dropped the ceilings to eight feet and removed all of the moldings and fireplaces. Williams and Nakib restored the moldings, opened the fireplaces, and replaced all the floors with unique parquet, composed of three kinds of wood.

Work began in 1996 and some incredible discoveries were made. Hidden beneath the low front hall ceiling lurked a magnificent coffered masterpiece. They retraced its central design, restoring the ceiling to its original glory.

Williams masterfully combined the couple's most beloved belongings in a comfortable yet bold red-lacquered library/cigar bar. She built bookcases to accommodate the wife's extensive book collection, and decorated the room with the wonderful eighteenth-century English furniture the husband had collected with his late wife.

The owner's insistence on a black dining room led to this spectacular result.

The most challenging room for Williams was the dining room. She had worked on the room twice before in this building, once with Sister Parrish and once with Albert Hadley. "It's almost too big and the windows are not centered. I'd seen both Parrish and Hadley struggle. Finally, I decided to create an oval where the fireplace is, and to use mirrored doors for storage. I was able to center the window on one wall and divide the room into three bays, allowing for a big round table or three smaller ones for entertaining. Since my client wanted the room to be black, we added columns, an eighteenth-century English white marble mantel, and a sparkling Russian chandelier to contrast with the dark walls." The couple was thrilled with Williams's solution since they often entertain.

The breakfast room hides the wife's work station and cookbooks behind painted doors. This room also boasts a ceiling painted with trompe l'oeil clouds and scalloped lattice.

Even more bookcases line the bedroom hall, which leads to the guest room. "No one wants to leave," says the wife. "The guest room is so cozy. Sometimes I think I run a boarding house!" The beautifully-painted four-poster bed would be reason enough to prolong a visit. The master bedroom holds a lovely Chippendale eighteenth-century bed from Sotheby's, adorned with English-style linens, Italian painted dressers found in London, and an eighteenth-century Venetian mirror. Delighted with the results, this happy couple appreciates Williams' vision. Her almost magical ability restored the apartment to the same beauty it possessed at the turn of the century.

OPPOSITE: *"We have beautiful southern and western exposures, which fill the room with light and wonderful views."*

ABOVE: *The guest room, complete with a fireplace and a four-poster bed, reflects the owner's southern heritage.*

A spectacular duplex

in one of the best buildings in New York, designed by the architect Rosario Candela in 1929, provoked a woman living abroad—a connoisseur of European furniture and an interior designer—to call in her dream team: the late, famed, French designer Henri Samuel, and the noted architect Thierry Despont. "My husband and I love to entertain," explains the worldly owner of this duplex.

The front hall, built to resemble cut limestone, was hand-grooved. The railing of the broad marble staircase was crafted in France.

RIGHT *and* OPPOSITE: *Visitors enter a virtual French country home. Inspiring this décor were sets of double doors handpainted with charming chateau scenes, once belonging to Samuel.*

In the hall, a nineteenth-century American mirror reflects a French Empire chandelier carved in the shape of grapes. Late eighteenth-century pineapple juicers sit on each end of a nineteenth-century French Empire sideboard.

"We had been looking at narrow townhouses, but one can never properly seat more than ten in one room. Then I was taken with the idea of a duplex. One could see the possibilities offered by such grand proportions." Imagining these possibilities, Samuel and Despont transformed the duplex's layout, knocking out walls, creating one long drawing room on the second floor, uncovering the stair windows in order to let in light, and reconfiguring the first floor. The project took one year, and was completed in 1985.

A large first floor space became a second sitting room. "It was impossible to use as a library. The light was too bright! So I thought, why not create a winter garden?" says the owner. "It grew from eighteenth-century painted canvas panels, from a Belgian chateau. We purchased them years before, at the Biennale des Antiquaires in Paris. They were so beautiful. We had no place for them then, but knew that one day we would use them."

RIGHT: *A detail of one of the lamps by the door in the winter garden.*

Creating a fantastical winter garden—in an otherwise classical apartment—was an adventure. The team first created a coffered dome painted with clouds. The walls were painted trompe l'oeil to resemble bamboo, but finding the ideal wall color was a challenge. "When you paint, you must see how it reads," she says. "[Samuel] would sit and stand in the room, observing the color from all angles, in the bright morning light, as well as in the afternoon. He studied it with lamplight. I learned from him. He always came himself, never sending an assistant. He was like a couturier, always fine-tuning details."

Resin was applied to create depth. Parquet de Versailles was installed and covered by a Russian nineteenth-century Bessarabian rug, full of flowers. A fanciful English porcelain mantle from 1815 holds eighteenth-century mother-of-pearl lanterns and a French eighteenth-century porcelain clock in the style of the Brighton Pavilion. A Russian chandelier from the same period hangs over nineteenth-century Danish chairs with their original passementerie trims. The coffee table was fashioned specially for Samuel, who worked with Giacometti on its design. Eighteenth-century French sconces and a console from the Wrightsman collection occupy one wall. Seventeenth-century Trapani coral objects, pillows covered in eighteenth-century handpainted Chinoiserie on silk, and pagoda-shaped lampshades with appliquéd butterflies are placed throughout.

The room is full of delightful detail. A needlepoint hamper—found on the Left Bank in Paris—is filled with gardenias, turning it into a giant jardinière scenting the air. In a window cage, lovebirds sing, plumage precisely matching the "garden's" celadon walls. Eye-level tree tops complete the effect. One can escape gray days here, where lunch is served at an elegantly set, small table next to a flickering fire. "Samuel was like an eighteenth-century decorator. He would give you a base, not choose everything himself. My husband and I found every piece in this room," she says, proudly surveying her garden.

OPPOSITE *and* ABOVE: *The dining room features raised Adam-style wall decoration, and Adam ballroom chairs and knife urns.*

Throwing open the doors to her blue and white dining room, one fully comprehends the apartment's classical appeal. On the floor rests a rug similar to one exhibited at Sir John Soane's Museum in London. A French rock-crystal chandelier, an English mirror and paneling—all from the eighteenth century—as well as a screen that once belonged to Daisy Fellowes, complete this elegant setting for the couple's frequent and lively dinner parties.

North of the United Nations

rises an imposing wall of dark glass: a forty-story tower in the International style, built in the 1960s. What drew Tom Armstrong, Director Emeritus of the Whitney Museum of American Art, to this skyscraper? "My wife was determined to have light and a view. We looked all over Park Avenue, where we once lived in a large traditional apartment, found nothing, and decided to look at U.N. Plaza."

ABOVE: *Green jade glass by Frederick Carder circa 1925, surrounds a painting by Jan Matulka, circa 1927, inspired by European modernism.*

OPPOSITE: *Mexican jug and double dish/angels/electric light by Andrew Ford, 1983, and Young Puma Sitting by Edward Kemeys, circa 1900, represent the diversity of American art the Armstrong's enjoy.*

When they finally found a smaller space with astonishing views, the couple naturally turned to their friend, noted designer Pamela Banker, with whom they had worked three times before. Following Banker's advice, they first reconfigured the space by opening two walls, tearing one down, and applying decorative moldings.

"We downscaled, giving the children the furniture they wanted and selling the rest at auction. Free to start from scratch, we commissioned a dining room table and several other pieces from contemporary furniture maker Harris Rubin."

Armstrong's glass collection holds center stage. He particularly admires Frederick Carder—founder of the Steuben Glass Company in the early twentieth century—who worked briefly in colored glass. "Carder made his colored pieces for only thirty years. I love the colors, the classical shapes, and the fact that it's one artist's accomplishment over a brief period." Especially at night Armstrong's glass collection shimmers, its green and pink tones complementing celadon cushions and walls.

"I'm a gardener, so most things I have are related to nature," Armstrong explains. The morning room walls (above) are covered with a series of four bold nineteenth-century chromolithographs by John Fisk Allen depicting the development of the Victoria lily. They are associated with contemporary work by Richard Baker, Andrew Masullo and Ray Parker. Chinese screens (opposite and following pages) evoking nature are mounted on the living room walls. The screens belonged to his mother-in-law. "We've had them in all our homes."

A glazed earthenware wall sculpture by Betty Woodman, Balustrade Relief Vase, #39, 1992, above the dining table by Harris Rubin, is one of three works by the artist in the apartment.

American art in general, in addition to the glass collection, defines this apartment. Ceramics by Andrew Lord and Betty Woodman adorn a dining room window. In the hall, paintings by Andrew Masullo—another contemporary artist —join works by Jan Matulka, a Czech-American painter and printmaker. In the library, an antique mirror reflects more Carder glass, and Betty Woodman sculpture. Mustard-striated walls offer a striking background for Wanda Gag's prints of American interiors from the 30s. An Andy Warhol "Marilyn" brightens the hall leading to Armstrong's dressing room. "Andy would give us gifts at Christmas of signed and inscribed prints," he explains.

The back hall holds a print of the Whitney Studio Club, where artists could pay a quarter and work from live models. Mabel Dwight's print shows Edward Hopper among a group of artists. In the front hall hang drawings by Rosela Hartman, which were exhibited at the Whitney in the 20s. Works by Joseph McCarthy, an untrained artist from the 50s, hang in the powder room and kitchen, along with a work by him composed as a comic strip, "Nudeo Rodeo". Vegetable-shaped cookie jars add to the eclectic mix. An inscribed Jasper Johns print celebrating his 1977 Whitney retrospective and a Robert Mapplethorpe photograph, a gift to the owners after his 1988 Whitney retrospective, decorate the husband's taupe-striped office.

The bedroom's green floral wallpaper brings nature inside. Taffeta curtains cascade beside the vast windows. Suspended above the river, overlooking the United Nations Rose Garden, Armstrong often sits in his favorite green chair, while his wife looks out from her desk, appreciating the late afternoon light. "It's my favorite place to look down the river. I love the sculptural quality of the UN and the shape of the Con-Ed building. It's a whole composition of straight lines and curves." A series of Audubon quadrupeds—a rabbit, raccoon, fox, and squirrel—cover one wall. Richard Baker's painting of thorny roses hangs over the desk, across from lithographs by Victoria Hutson Huntley and additional prints by Wanda Gag. Lilac Carder glass decorates the coffee table.

"This project went fast. I don't like things to linger," Armstrong explains. Everything had a destination. It's interesting to move. You learn to use space better. We love our views!"

OPPOSITE: *Wendell Castle's signed wooden desk and chair from 1973, inscribed from Tom to his wife Bunty, sit on a persimmon rug in the library.*

Perched high above upper Park Avenue,

In the hallway Biggs filled a black japanned cabinet with eighteenth-century "Fishscale" Spode plates and objects. Buying them, many years ago, turned her into an incurable collector.

this unique triplex wrap-around-terraced penthouse seemed a worthy project for its owner, Friederike Kemp Biggs, an accomplished interior designer. Built in 1929 by renowned architect Rosario Candela, this grand apartment is cozy, not cavernous. "It feels like a house, not an ordinary apartment, with tons of light."

RIGHT: *Off the hallway Biggs created a study and turned an ajoining bathroom into a library.*

OPPOSITE: *Inspired by a famous Thomas Jefferson quote, Biggs stenciled the phrase "I cannot live without my books" onto the library wall. Biggs used the word "my" in Jefferson's quote because, as she says, "my husband is very possessive of his books."*

After finding the original floor plans, Biggs transformed a bathroom into an elegant library to make room for her husband's many cherished volumes. She also hung rice paper paintings of Chinese adults and children at play by Louise Ashe Lord, the daughter of a nineteenth-century English missionary to China. The wall also features a framed, embroidered children's coat, a Chinese antique, reflecting years Biggs spent as a girl in Taipei.

Chinoiserie abounds in this apartment, particularly in the foyer. The chinoiserie theme is also echoed in designs painted around the foyer window.

LEFT: *At one end of the entrance hall, stands a seven-foot birdcage painted black and gold in the Regency style, flanked by a collection of tall nineteenth-century Chinese Export blue and white vases.*

ABOVE: *The enormous windows with spectacular views of sunrise and sunset drew Biggs to the space. The furniture shows Biggs' love of oriental art, while two panels of Noh costumes are hung to the right of the fireplace.*

OPPOSITE TOP: *A huge Japanese screen hangs on the living room wall.*

Panoramic views of the city create a perfect backdrop for collections of blue and white porcelain, the dishes and tureens including Delft, Spode, and Chinese Export pieces, collected on world travel. Lacquerware and chairs from many periods are arranged with brilliant symmetry. "We each brought special things to this apartment. My husband brought his Rembrandt, his Churchill collection of books and paintings, his mother's needlepoint, and porcelain birds made by the English artist Dorothy Doughty. It's just a hodgepodge," says Biggs modestly. Yet the military precision with which she organizes her massive collections helps make this apartment so engaging.

Three arrangements of furniture artfully divide the living room, maximizing seating space. Glass cabinets hold gleaming collections of peach Spode. The walls are covered with Noh costumes and a painting by Paul Maze—Winston Churchill's close friend and art teacher. The living room is especially magical when the Park Avenue Christmas tree-lighting ceremony takes place—friends gather here to see the giant ribbon of light on the street below.

ABOVE: *A grand piano hides a tiny chair painted with the names of Biggs' grandchildren.*

In the center of the dramatic dining room, lined with the original painted panels, is one of the most unusual pieces: a birdcage hung in lieu of a chandelier—birdcases are found in almost every room in the apartment. Surrounding what the owner calls her "Chipplewhite" table are the couple's collections of crystal balls, candle sticks, silver vases, and thumbnail punch bowls, often filled with cranberries. Guests are bedazzled as the moon rises on cue through the dining room's giant central window, seen (right) with part of the silver collection.

ABOVE: *A secret staircase leads upstairs from the kitchen to the boys' rooms. The space under the staircase was cleverly used to house a second refrigerator, hidden behind doors painted trompe l'oeil. In the painting, the labels on the bottles of wine were completed with the Biggs family crest.*
LEFT: *More blue-and-white porcelain fills the kitchen, as do the signature birdcages.*

The walls of Friederike's office are lined with blue-and-white porcelain, prints, and engravings, while the tables are laden with fabric samples and books. Her desk is an English breakfast table. Biggs applied her design acumen turning a wine cellarette into a file cabinet.

The kitchen is a tour de force, painted by Christian Brandner. "Give us fruit and vegetables," Biggs commanded, and Brander did! Monkeys and birdcages swing beside ovens and ranges. Ceramic Delft bird tiles and original cabinets, painted with a squeegee, vie for space. A cork-filled basket testifies to the bottles of wine shared around the family kitchen table. "It reminds us of many good times."

Her office, a sea of organized clutter, proves that brilliance can spring from chaos. Biggs knows where every paper is buried, and finds time to sit by the window and watch the apple tree on the terrace grow. Blue and white porcelain, botanical prints, and frames of silver and shell cover any empty space. A delicate border of leaves trails across the ceiling.

The master bedroom, at the head of a small stair, offers quiet. "It's my escape hatch," says the owner. "We can see the sunset from our bed." On the walls hang Bessler botanical prints, and the carpet is strewn with woven flowers, mirroring the flower-filled terrace outside. This room truly represents the couple's private paradise above the city.

OPPOSITE: *The sconces in the dressing room were once firebacks: Biggs had them made into lights.*

ABOVE: *The love seat at the foot of the bed was once broken in half. Biggs had it carefully restored and rebuilt.*

Views from Central Park South

RIGHT: *Inspired by designer Billy Baldwin's famous azure and white room at La Fiorentina—a villa in the south of France—the living room's focal point is a panoramic view of Central Park.*

OPPOSITE: *Inside the living room stands an eighteenth-century walnut Italian tall case clock was purchased in London. To the left is a Marino Marini bronze, a horse, "Cavallo." Above the door is Picasso's painting, "Jeune Femme en Bleue Robe Ciel."*

as green and beautiful as this, similar to the ones the owners so enjoy in the country, were hard to find. The couple who live here once wondered if they could find the perfect space to accommodate their growing family, display their fantastic art, and continue entertaining on a grand scale.

The sweeping, dramatic space Easton created suits the powerful series of paintings of women by Pablo Picasso, the bold geometry of Richard Diebenkorn, and the large colorful works by Leger and Braque that the husband loves to collect. A Japanese lacquer trunk with metal mounts, a Marino Marini bronze horse, Genovese eighteenth-century painted consoles and a collection of blue and white charger plates fill the vast space.

RIGHT:
Plates by Picasso lend charm and humor to the room.

It took imagination, two years, and the help of architect and interior designer David Easton to do the job. Easton reconfigured the space, which had been created out of five apartments by the previous owner. Every wall was taken down, until one could see from one end of the space to another. Eighteenth-century boiseries and parquet were carefully moved, revealing the living room's two-story ceiling and original arched windows.

A blue-and-white rug, specially woven in Portugal, at the Madeira Gobelins factory, follows ancient techniques using three types of knots, adding texture and depth to the bold pattern. "We were inspired by a visit to a Lisbon museum where we saw antique rugs with raised and layered stitches. The technique provides the texture needed for a rug big enough to fill an 18 x 32 foot room with 18 foot ceilings," says Easton. "The high ceiling was lowered 3 or 4 inches to install air-conditioning. The walls are covered with an ancient European plastering technique involving rough-cast paint, ground stone and plaster and many coats of white on white to create a textured effect, lending a warm country feel to the room, subtly reflecting the light."

"The project took two years and blood, sweat and tears," according to the wife, "but it was worth it." Not many apartments offer views from the Hudson to the East River.

The living room is often used for receptions, such as Central Park Conservancy breakfasts and political events. "When an organization needs a place to host receptions, we'll help," says the wife, graciously.

RIGHT: *In the vestibule stands a nineteenth-century English pagoda. Above the flowers in the hallway hangs "La Route," a painting by Paul Cezanne.*

"Wonderful art, views like a 30's Hollywood picture, very Fred Astaire and Ginger Rogers, but in a quality building," adds Easton. "You could count few apartments like this in Manhattan. The living room gives you a great feeling and then you can tippy-toe on out to the terrace!" Glazing the English mantel to blend in with the walls and choosing subtle window treatments, like clean French poles of iron or steel to hang curtains, Easton emphasized the views.

OPPOSITE: *On either side of the window sits a pair of blue and white cast iron French jardinières. Decorating the walls are paintings by two Fauves, Kees Van Dongen and Maurice de Vlaminck. In the center of the hall stands an Irish brass-mounted giltwood center table from the period of William IV, (1765-1837).*
LEFT: *In the power room off the hallway, Salvador Dali's "Instrument Masochiste" is reflected in a continental neoclassical giltwood silver gilt and red velvet mirror.*

PREVIOUS PAGES: *The intimate dining room has a curved octagonal ceiling. Easton specially commissioned Gracie to rescale and hand paint a copy of an antique wallpaper covered with birds and flowers. Russian ivory pagodas and an Irish Georgian sideboard complete the room.*

LEFT: *The kitchen, large enough to support the hospitality of this philanthropic duo, has a cork floor, stripped-pine cabinets and white-tiled counter tops surrounding a central island.*
BELOW: *Looking across the kitchen island, one sees into the family room, a cozy library, "Just for us!" says the wife. Under the watchful eyes of Emil Nolde's "Fishing Boat- Red Sky," the family enjoys television and films on a forty-four inch flat screen TV.*

ABOVE: *The couple took the original dining room, which held the former owner's Monet, "Water Lilies," and turned it into their bedroom. "It hurt to tear out the paneled dining room, but we needed a bath tub." Large closets were also added, making room for multicolored piles of neatly folded sweaters.*
OPPOSITE: *The tiled master bath, adapted from mosaics found at Pompeii, offers a breathtaking view of Central Park from its window-side tub. The brass taps, a series of sea horses and dolphins, belonged to the former owner but seem made for this decor.*

A king-sized tester bed, draped with off-white raw silk, lined in melon batik, flanked by two hand-painted side tables faces glorious views of the park. A soft-green painted English chest of drawers sits beneath a bookcase filled with eighteenth-century Chelsea porcelain leaf and lettuce plates, vegetable-shaped tureens, and eighteenth-century Sceaux faience vegetables. A welcoming fireplace faces the bed. A cozy love seat and a comfortable peach-upholstered arm chair sit on an off-white rug, crossed with raised-coral stitches, creating a comfortable corner where the couple enjoy curling up and reading. Subtle plaid-glazed peach walls and delicate curtains enhance the view. An eighteenth-century black lacquer secretary holds English porcelain and a Clare Potter porcelain Primula, and is flanked by a pair of red-lacquer Queen Anne claw-footed side chairs. When the view is not enough, a push of a bedside button sends the over-mantle mirror rising into the ceiling, revealing a hidden television inside the gilt frame.

Stepping inside their apartment, one sees that the couple have succeeded in creating the country in the city.

A vast collection of modern art

is superbly displayed here in a setting tailormade by the owners for it. To achieve this, they hired the architect Oscar Shamami-an and the designer Brian Murphy.

ABOVE: *One enters the hallway through a huge, specially cast steel door.*

ABOVE AND PRECEDING PAGES: *The smaller of the two living rooms (above), both of which overlook Central Park, holds works by Kandinsky, Leger, Dubuffet, Giacometti, and Gorky. The larger living room (preceding pages) is anchored by a double-sided sofa in its center and displayed are larger-scale works by Rothko, Pollock, Newman, and Still. French chairs from the collection of Madeleine Castaing flank an eighteenth-century silver-leafed Italian coffee table.*

LEFT and RIGHT: *The collection ranges from impressive works by Alberto Giacometti (seen at the end of the hallway) and Christo to a pair of Oldenberg sneakers—playfully tucked under an eighteenth-century inlaid library table placed in the center of the hall in front of two works by Francis Bacon.*

ABOVE: *Antique "curtains" of carved wood frame the windows in the dining room. A large painting by Twombly hangs between two wooden cellarettes shaped like urns.*
OPPOSITE: *"Putting our furniture in a different context made it fresh and new for us," the wife says.*

The couple explains: "We reallocated a large proportion of the seventy-five hundred square foot apartment for public space. Ceilings were lowered to make room for sophisticated and unobtrusive art lighting. Pocket doors, used strategically, eliminated the problem of doors folding back and obscuring paintings. Nearly every interior wall was knocked down and repositioned." Murphy understood his clients' preference for classical detail—maintaining moldings on ceilings wherever possible—but left the walls unadorned.

The couple began collecting in 1970, starting with Abstract Expressionism and Pop Art. During the 80s, they shifted their focus to Contemporary Art, scouring Soho galleries every weekend for new talent. In the 90s, however, they returned to their roots, acquiring older pieces. Their favorite works include a 1964 Andy Warhol entitled "The Week That Was," a poignant reminder of JFK's assassination, and a Miro portrait from the 1930s. Sitting in any room, surrounded by such great works, the lady of the house says, "There is no bad seat in the house!" One would have to agree.

RIGHT *and* ABOVE: *The majestic dining
room, with works by Lichtenstein, Pollock,
de Kooning, and Twombly, was created by
incorporating the former breakfast room
into the main space. Columns gracefully
camouflage differing ceiling heights. "We
weren't afraid to attack a grand apartment
that had no air conditioning. We fixed five
fireplaces, raised doorways, and used pocket
doors so that nothing covered our art or
wasted space," says the wife.*

ABOVE and RIGHT: *The faux-tortoiseshell library was inspired by a room designed by the late Henri Samuel, the noted French decorator, for Sao Schlumberger. Silver tea paper covers the ceiling, while book-lined walls contain reference works on the couple's favorite artists. The shelves are punctuated by the work of Gerhard Richter, Jasper Johns, and Anthony Gormley.*

Above the 59th Street Bridge

lay the extraordinary apartment of Annenberg heiress Janet Hooker. In the spring of 2000, the current owner, Lisa Perry, learned it was for sale. The apartment had a rich history—even serving as the scene of a famous 1958 *Life Magazine* cover shot of the era's socialites.

A trip from the building's traditional lobby to Perry's bright entrance hall—covered with works by Wesselman, Lichtenstein, Warhol, and Raysse—is like a trip to outer space. A circle motif resonates from room to room: flanking the front door are lacquered door panels with glass portholes. In the powder room, a four-paneled scene of changing, beguiling multicolored lights illuminates a Jeff Koons mirror.

The original coffered ceiling and eight foot French doors were removed and replaced with a fifteen foot seamless-vaulted ceiling. Below lies the living room designed by Ingrao: "a conversation pit" with undulating sofas dotted with graphic, black-and-white op-art pillows. A giant Lichtenstein, a Rauschenberg, a Jim Dine, and a Vasarely adorn the walls. Oldenberg's "Soft Fur Good Humors" lies horizontal under glass, serving as a coffee table. Vintage 60s Italian furniture and a shag rug complete the picture: Perry has certainly achieved her vision of "a cool airport lounge," framed by twelve-foot glass doors revealing spectacular views and the terrace.

Mr. Guest's mother, Amy Phipps, had first lived here. Her grandfather's Fifth Avenue chateau, demolished in 1927, made way for the new apartment house. Phipps preserved the gilded-coffered ceilings and white marble floors from her grandfather's mansion and installed them in her new apartment. The new residence, built by Candela and Cross and Cross, became legendary itself, with two grand ballrooms and magnificent views of the East River.

"It was so old world and so big. It stunned us," says Perry. "It looked like a mini Versailles. I'm a modern girl and wanted lots of light. I brought in Tony Ingrao, a designer friend, and David Piscuskas, of 1100 Architect, because of his clean vision. Both designers were struck by the fact that inner corridors blocked out the afternoon light. Pending permission to change the windows and interior walls, we said 'Let's Do It!'"

Though the apartment had been untouched for thirty years, the building's board permitted Perry to remove elaborate moldings, nine fireplaces, and elegant ballrooms. A year-and-a half later, a totally modern space was created out of the seven-thousand square foot U-shaped penthouse with six-thousand foot terraces. "It's futuristic," says Perry. "It's the Jetsons!"

The library is red, white, and black, right down to the colored M&M's and coffee table in the shape of dice. Color-coded books line the walls: a reference library dedicated to study of the couple's collections. A Lucite guitar, rumored to have been used by the Rolling Stones, and Beatles memorabilia hang above a red couch and black and white rug.

OPPOSITE: *In the dining room—originally the kitchen—guests congregate at the round, steel dining table surrounded by neon orange chairs and a neon orange ceiling light. These fluorescent colors glow in the dark, setting off Bridget Riley's black-and-white Op-art as well as Wesselman's "Mouth 16."*

LEFT: *A bubble-gum pink storage cube and pink platform bed niche for the couple's daughter in her bedroom.*

The guest room is decorated with Marimekko shades and sheets.

ABOVE: *The kitchen, formerly a Georgian-paneled dining room, stands at center stage. Warhol-inspired cups and mugs fill glass cabinets. A giant stainless steel egg beater hangs from the ceiling above an Eero Saarinen table and chairs.*

"Love," Robert Indiana's stainless steel sculpture, can also be seen as a mosaic outside, illuminated at night. The apartment is a tribute to the artists and stylemakers of the 60s and 70s: a showcase for Pop Art icons, including furniture by Verner Panton and art by Warhol, Oldenberg, and Rauschenberg.

The media room is furnished with Cappellini curved chairs covered in Pucci-print, leather and Lucite coffee tables, hot pink pillows, a black and brown rug, a built-in seven-foot-wide projection screen, and a Robert Indiana sculpture entitled "Love". The sofa fabric is the work of Alexandre Girard, a mid-century designer. Along with Gae Aulenti's steel-walled 70s Milanese apartment, Girard's work has been a great influence on Perry's design concepts.

In the north hall sits a Warhol soup can, a piece by Richard Hamilton—a father of Pop Art working in the United Kingdom in the 60s—as well as Mel Ramos pinups and Oldenberg's "Alphabet Good Humor."

Perry, a child of the sixties, is dedicated to the progressive political and social ideas of the period as well as its art. A staunch Democrat with progressive sensibility, she responds to the art and music of the period, favoring Bob Dylan, the Beatles, Marimekko fabrics and mod clothes. This supermodern apartment brings a smile to the face of all who enter. What a surprise this bold creation would be to its former owners!

*Perry's dressing room boasts built-in, floor-to-ceiling closets, lined
in blindingly white lacquer squares. A stylist's dream, Perry's closet
is filled with vintage 60s Courrèges, Cardin, Gernreich, and Pucci
clothes. The room also includes a circular vinyl ottoman with
Lucite legs, standing on a black and white graphic rug.*

Perry calls the master bedroom "Austin Powers meets Barbarella." The headboard's vinyl and Lucite concentric circles are repeated in the pattern of the rug. White walls set off the 1959 Lavergne Lucite Lily chair. Photographs from the 60s by Klein, Dahl-Wolfe and Horst adorn the walls, but Wesselman's giant spread-legged "Great American Nude" truly dominates the room.

At the foot of the bed stands a white lacquered island holding books and a giant pop-up projection screen. At night the 59th Street bridge can be clearly seen from the his-and-her white chaise lounges.

"Everything about this Fifth Avenue apartment

attracted me," explains elegant philanthropist Carroll Petrie, who moved into this spectacular Fifth Avenue residence—in a 1931 Rosario Candela building—over twenty years ago, with her late husband Milton. "Having lived in Europe and Hong Kong, it was time for my children to grow up American. This was to be their base."

PRECEDING PAGES: *The drawing room contains outstanding pieces including a fine pair of George III satinwood bookcase cabinets with lemonwood inlay, which hold a collection of early nineteenth-century English Davenport porcelain. On the fireplace wall are a pair of Hubert Robert landscapes and a George Romney portrait, circa 1780.*
LEFT: *The custom-made carpet from Hamot, in Paris, is a garden of flowers, from an original design by David Easton.*
BELOW: *Above the large blue silk sofa in the drawing room is a mid-eighteenth-century George III carved gilt wood oval mirror, surrounded by four Chinese Export, enamel-decorated porcelain, ormolu-mounted sconces. An early nineteenth-century Swedish chandelier hangs from the ceiling.*
RIGHT: *John Christensen recently redecorated the card room. Its walls formerly plush red, the space is now white-on-white, the walls now covered with game felled by Carroll while trekking through Outer Mongolia, Afghanistan, and Kenya: the antlers of a Marco Polo sheep, an Oryx, a Waterbuck, a Warthog, and a Markhor, or goat. "It was quite an adventure!" Now these souvenirs surround her, along with a giant American flag, Andy Warhol flowers—autographed by him on the back—and a ceiling covered in silver tea-paper. "I started playing cards on Sunday night at Elsa Maxwell's and have played ever since."*

Entering the drawing room, tuberose scents the air, orchids abound, and vases are filled with fragrant blossoms in shades of pink. Outside is another garden: Central Park, offering a cheerful backdrop to this welcoming room, with its billowing pink and apricot-striped taffeta curtains. An enchanting painting by George Romney, "Lady in Blue Hat," hangs above the mantel. A pair of Hubert Robert paintings of Roman ruins flank the fireplace. Two eighteenth-century French faience lions perch on a pair of gilt wood consoles with lapis lazuli tops.

The room, overlooking Central Park, had originally stretched along the length of the apartment. Petrie enlisted David Easton to transform this space, in order to form a small library and card room. Easton—and his assistant at the time, John Christensen—respected their client's love of pastels, creating yellow glazed faux-bois walls to reflect both sunlight and moonlight.

In the gallery a fine Regency carved gilt wood console table with a Sienna marble top from Godmersham Park in Kent, where Jane Austen spent time, were found by the couple at auction in England. Warm, unexpected touches, such as pink lining in the floor-to-ceiling bookcases filled with antique leather-bound books—mixed with early nineteenth-century Worcester square plates and a pair of English Bengal Tiger fruit coolers—serve as a reminder that this is the residence of a Southern woman who loves the flattering glow of pink.

Christensen knows that dining rooms can become wasted space, so this one is filled with a sofa and cabinets. The room also contains an eighteenth-century Queen Anne walnut bureau bookcase with upper-mirrored doors.

ABOVE: A pair of eighteenth-century Italian carved gilt wood mirrors—each over seven feet tall—add drama to the room.

Her latest creation, her dining room, is glazed a pale pink. "Most flattering to the skin, don't you agree?" Below a ceiling covered in clouds, up to thirty guests can be seated at tables skirted to the floor with striped taffeta. Gracious and hospitable, with a pale cashmere sweater tossed casually over her shoulders, Petrie continues to be involved in the New York charities that meant so much to her husband and still add meaning to her busy life.

In this midtown apartment

one could reasonably ask what to do with thirteen-foot ceilings? With seven thousand square feet on three floors? With two terraces? Connect the floors with a winding staircase, cover the walls with an extraordinary collection of art, find fanciful 1940s furniture. Keep it warm and cozy with lavish curtains and miles of carpet, give a special floor over to your children complete with its own playground, and enjoy life!

In the living room Khmer treasures such as a Buddha head, discovered on the couple's honeymoon in Southeast Asia, rest beside a collection of photography books in specially-designed Plexiglas cases. Ed Ruscha's "War Surplus" joins a painting by Francis Bacon. The table in the foreground is a Dorothy Draper 30s design in black lacquer, now covered in goatskin with its legs lightened.

In the sprawling living room, painted in a soft palette, hangs Rauschenberg's 1961 masterpiece, "Third Time Painting," and Ellsworth Kelly's "Red blue," along with works by Rothko and Lichtenstein. Sweeping silk-taffeta curtains studded with Swarovski crystals, inspired by a pearl-studded pillow, are typical of the decorative touches Tenenbaum favors. "I just love big curtains!" she says.

Ann Tenenbaum and her financier husband, Tom Lee, started married life by renting two floors in a venerable 1929 building where Orson Welles once lived. Close to Sutton Place, the building was originally built to house artists' studios.

The birth of two sons changed the couple's needs. They could no longer accommodate both their passion for collecting art and their growing family on two floors. Discovering that their apartment had previously been part of a triplex, Tenenbaum and Lee convinced the owner to vacate the floor below and sell all three floors to them. Recreating the triplex was daunting. Finally, after two years of renovation with the help of designer DD Allen, they moved back in the fall of 1999.

OPPOSITE: *In the dining room a giant Dale Chihuly glass sculpture of leaf and shell forms shimmers as a chandelier, illuminated by pin lights from above.*

The adjoining library/bar/screening room boasts large paintings by Gerhard Richter, Sigmar Polke, and Stuart Davis, a Diane Arbus photograph, a Roy Lichtenstein drawing, silver leaf doors, and a tea paper ceiling.

Off the hallway, the dining room, featuring a table covered in cracked-surfboard paint and waxed to just the right color of turquoise, sits surrounded by white dinner chairs with beaded backs. Rock crystal accessories adorn the room. Pale violet walls provide a glossy background for an Andy Warhol self-portrait, an Agnes Martin, and a Mondrian.

An antique rug and maroon silk curtains lined with lime green velvet absorb dinner-party clamor.

LEFT: *A sinuous upholstered seat curves along the screening room's mohair walls.*
RIGHT: *A Tiffany-blue powder room with a jeweled shade-pull holds a shagreen sink.*

At the base of the pearl grey carpeted, twisting staircase which connects the three floors, a two-thousand-year-old Egyptian head stands as sentry. Dangling down the winding staircase hangs a Verner Panton light fixture of eight hanging pods.

Tenenbaum always wanted a rose-colored bedroom. "I dreamed about it. That was the starting point. I wanted an apartment that wasn't like everyone else's: No wood paneling, no wooden floors." Her urge to be different may have come from her family. She grew up in Savannah, Georgia where her parents lived in an 1870's house in the center of the city. "They turned it into a modern house that made most people in Savannah freak out, although it was featured on the cover of *House Beautiful* in 1974."

Upstairs, Tenenbaum achieved her dream of a rose-colored bedroom. A tufted sofa and lilac cashmere bed-throw affirm her need for Southern comfort. Tom's masculine den and a blue and gold guest room with bubble-quilted walls and headboard complete the second floor.

A Jean Royere lamp standing in the corner joins work by Georg Baselitz and the Monet in the bedroom.

ABOVE: *Tenenbaum and Lee's passion for art brought them together. On their first date, Lee impressed his young wife-to-be by taking her to an auction, where he bought a Monet that now now hangs opposite their bed.*

A renowned architect decided

to take himself and his wife on as clients. What happened? Charles Gwathmey did just that twelve years ago, when he moved to a higher floor in the same Rosario Candela building where he and his wife, Bette-Ann, had raised their family. Gutting a traditional, three bedroom apartment measuring twenty-five hundred square feet he created a dramatic loft for two.

LEFT: *Ambient light articulates the carved walls, while mono-points highlight the art. Panels of glass imply space beyond. "The bedroom is behind, but it is not perceived from the main hall," Gwathmey explains. "You're looking through the space, guided by light. Psychologically, movement pulls you towards the far wall, which is tilted toward the marble floor." Above the bench in the hallway hangs Josef Alber's series "Homage to The Square."*

ABOVE: *A Josef Hoffmann table stands in the entry hall with one of his vases. Above it hangs Andre Kertesz's photograph of Mondrian's studio.*

ABOVE: *Bette-Ann's desk, facing the Central Park Reservoir, maximizes the view. "We love being at the top of the trees," she says. Hidden shades and lights sit above the openings of window frames, making the walls seem thicker.* FOLLOWING PAGES: *In the living area, a black and white rug, made in Vienna from a Hoffman design, creates a sitting space. A Louis Sullivan plaster casting from the Garrick Theatre stands above a stone fireplace centered in a canted wall.*

"There are two possibilities when architects do their own spaces," he explains. "You can try to do everything you could not do for clients, or use it to experiment, exploring things you think are urgent at that time. My idea was to create a space that feels as if it had been carved from a solid. Everything is framed and layered. The beige marble floor rotates off the building axis, while the bleached maple flooring throughout is parallel to the park. It's about object and frame. Every space is an object in a found frame defined by floor and ceiling articulation."

Entering the curving entry gallery, formerly a narrow hall, one is pulled forward by the giant sweep of ceiling which follows the turning floor. "What's left is what is essential," the architect points out. "Like a yacht, every inch is used." The stainless-steel entry hall door, brushed with sandblasted insets, picks up graphic squares from a Josef Hoffmann table, as do the chair rail and wooden doors separating the master bedroom from the open space ahead—subtly divided into three areas. Josef Albers's ten-picture series, "Homage to the Square," adds color and further geometry.

Originally, the apartment was painted shades of taupe and gray. Bette-Ann suggested painting the entire space white. "It made the space feel bigger and different, more carved and monolithic. For me everything is about reassessing what not to do." The white palette provides a perfect backdrop for Le Corbusier chairs the architect bought in 1962, while living in Paris as a Fulbright scholar.

Between the living and library areas stands what Gwathmey calls an "experiment in Cubist assemblage sculpture furniture: a room divider, meant to be a counterpoint to all the traditional objects in the apartment." "Othellia," painted by Robert Gwathmey, the architect's father, hangs in the library, along with a photograph from his son, adding warmth. According to Bette-Ann, "the photos are gifts, a family tradition—full of meaning and very personal."

BELOW: The dining area, set in its marble "frame," holds Thonet prototype chairs surrounding an original Gwathmey-designed table. A Sally Mann photograph covers one wall, joining an Ingres poster, a photo by Paul Strand, a drawing by Michael Graves, a Le Corbusier ink drawing, and a birdhouse Gwathmey designed for the Parrish Museum in Southampton.

The bedroom's curved ceiling and built-in cabinets and doors add depth, creating cross-axial symmetry. A maple bed and natural wool carpeting—the color of a grey flannel suit—pick up the neutral palette, serving to emphasize the view. Between the exposed windows rest a Thonet rocker and another Robert Gwathmey painting. Double-lattice louvers cover the radiators. His-and-her dressing rooms and marble bathrooms, with onyx sinks, flank the room. Each has windows on the park.

Photographs by Arnold Newman of Modigliani and Stravinsky connect the bar and pantry—which remain from the original apartment—to the new stainless steel, cherry wood, and marble-floored kitchen. A frosted grid on the kitchen window filters light, gives a sense of privacy while offering a sense of the beyond.

"The apartment feels very open, yet private," Bette-Ann says. "After thirty years together, the apartment reflects a big part of our lives. I was the client working with Charles' art and creativity. We went over the drawings together. It is uncluttered. Objects matter, they are not decorations. We love the pieces we have. The photos are gifts, a family tradition. They are full of meaning and very personal. It is history for us, all the things we've collected. It's exciting and romantic for the two of us to live in Charles' architecture. Its sophistication epitomizes New York and our neighborhood."

"I am interested in Secessionist Arts and Crafts," says Gwathmey, particularly the transition period around 1905, still modern, articulated, well-detailed, craft-oriented and architectural." Even the kitchen stool, designed by Gwathmey, refers to Secessionist furniture.

Superb views of Central Park

from this light-filled Fifth Avenue duplex, with its magnificent double-storied library, captured the fancy of two European-born philanthropists, a couple who generously support music, education, and the arts in New York.

Before moving in, in 1989, the couple removed columns in the living room, renovated the kitchen, took out the wall-to-wall carpeting, and completely redesigned the upstairs baths and bedrooms. Soon the couple were happily ensconced, giving the musicales they adore.

The broadly eclectic tone of the home reflects the couple's extensive travels. Alongside Italian, German and Austrian polychrome church art is Chagall's "The Kiss." The room's delightful mix also includes Chinese porcelain figures, a sixteenth-century wood carving representing the four seasons, a Swedish tall case clock—circa 1750— that winds backwards, three Bela Kadar paintings, and English Georgian and Regency furniture.

In the entrance hall, guests are welcomed by two Chinese terracotta horses that date back to the sixth century B.C.E., while paintings by Hungarian and Austrian avant-garde artists, who lived and worked with Picasso in the 1920s, hang nearby. Pissaro's "Paysanne Assise et Enfant" hangs above the horses.

Between the living room and dining room sits the imposing, while inviting and supremely tranquil, library. Warm, wood-paneled bookshelves rise twenty feet to the ceiling. Green sofas beckon one to read and relax, or listen to music. A seventeenth-century Dutch tapestry, a Matisse, and a Picasso drawing of a satyr adorn the room. Perched in an upper window is a metal sculpture by a contemporary German artist, Erik Engelbrecht. The room also includes the couple's collection of paperweights, English walking sticks, and Herend china objects. Some of these pieces are displayed on a triple-tiered table, itself a work of art. In addition there is a sculpture by Parisian artist Anna Stein.

Crossing through the library, one enters a cozy yet elegant dining room, which comfortably seats fourteen, the setting of many entertaining, spirited dinner parties. Textures of marble and damask, and a cushioned banquette—all in shades of green—create a feeling of enveloping warmth. A canopy of draped beige silk radiates from a golden Italian antique chandelier. Ming terracotta figures and a pitcher rest on the windowsill. An air conditioned wine cellar is visible from the dining room.

Ascending the staircase, which rises from the marble-floored foyer to the couple's private quarters, one walks up past a painting by Edwina Sandys, and approaches the husband's desk at the head of the stairs. Neatly organized, the desk is surrounded by architectural drawings suitable for an engineer.

Over the fireplace in the master bedroom hangs a piece by Istvan Csok, a Hungarian avant-garde painter. A beige floral chintz covers the sleigh-bed. Matching curtains rest on a pale lavender, floral needlepoint rug from Portugal.

The guest room's two canopied beds, covered in Provencal terracotta fabric, provide an inviting respite from the bustling city.

The walls of the staircase are decorated with a set of 1810 fashion plates by Horace Vernet. These pieces depict daredevil youths—"Incroyables et Merveilleuses"—who dressed up as dandies to bring back glamour after the French Revolution.

A Venetian mask by Angela Cummings, once worn to a costume ball at the Philharmonic, looks on from the wall of the dressing room.

The dressing room boasts a custom-made two-sided dressing table/desk, crafted by German sculptor Christina Engelbrecht. Framed family photographs cover all the surfaces in this room, which also includes a portrait of the lady of the house by Gladys Perint Palmer. Collections of perfume bottles glisten in a marble and mirrored bathroom next door.

"Everything in this apartment has a meaning. Nothing is for show. That's our style!" says the proud owner, surveying the space she decorated herself.

The owner of this majestic apartment

was among the first clients of the late, legendary designer Mark Hampton. The space boasts a vestibule with fine original plasterwork, a barrel-vaulted ceiling with octagonal coffers in the style of Robert Adam, elaborate carved mantels and moldings, and paneling and door surrounds by Rosario Candela—who had also designed the building.

LEFT: *In the entrance hall, trompe l'oeil cream and beige marbleized panels, by Robert Jackson, sit between Candela's columns.*

ABOVE: *Hampton had the walls of the vestibule painted to resemble stone blocks, like those one would find on the exterior of a house.*

ABOVE, RIGHT *and* INSET: *In the living room, one finds Italian neo-classical side tables and extraordinary Boulle Louis XIV marquetry pedestals from Versailles, placed between the windows. "We valued the depth of Mark's knowledge and authority. His sure hand allowed us to create a Continental mix—placing our French Regence mirror, Russian settee, Chinese lacquer tables, Italian Lavinia Fontana Madonna from the 1600s, and second-century Roman torso in this Georgian-detailed room with confidence." Accents of ebony and Louis XVI gueridons punctuate the room's decor.*

Originally, Hampton had given the apartment a classical Georgian treatment, complete with Chippendale furniture. Years later, his clients "wanted a complete change. Our vision was to create something Italian and neo-classical. In the eighties everyone wanted Mark to do the English Country look, but he was thrilled to stretch to another dimension. The three of us went on European shopping trips together. Traveling with Mark was like getting a Masters in Art History."

A nineteenth-century Italian Neo-classical statue of Penelope welcomes guests in the vestibule, while on the wall of the vestibule hangs an English Regency mirror, decorated with dolphins.

Entering the grand front hall, the powerful geometric design of the black, beige, and white marble floor draws one's eye to a marble statue from first-century Rome. The woman's draped, white figure is flanked by spiral topiaries and a pair of eighteenth-century English gilt benches, which are illuminated by early nineteenth-century Italian chandeliers.

In the dining room—designed for formal dinners—a collection of early nineteenth-century Regency silver by England's royal silversmith, Paul Storr, glistens under the light of a crystal chandelier. The Georgian detailing coexists beautifully with the Regency dining table and chairs. The border of the Regency console echoes the Greek key motif on the wainscoting. Italian eighteenth-century marble urns and a mirror reflect the Giovanni Paolo Panini Old Master paintings and seventeenth century bronze of Aurora rising from the sea.

*The library. Horse sculptures—including an early seventeenth-
century Giambologna bronze, a twentieth-century Degas bronze,
and an Etruscan rider—reflect the owners' equestrian interests.*

The library, with its shallow barrel-vaulted ceiling, was stripped down to the original pine. An eighteenth-century Pompeo Batoni painting of an English gentleman on the Grand Tour sits above an English Regency desk. Above the original Sienna marble fireplace hangs a Hubert Robert capriccio painting.

The couple's private quarters are restrained and comfortable. A Louis XVI desk supports an English Regency dolphin lamp. A nineteenth-century French sculpture rests between the trellised curtains, which are tied back with delicate flowers. An Italian neoclassical alabaster statue of the three graces overlooks the bed, with its graceful pediment. Arches, pilasters, mirrors, and a vaulted ceiling were added to the master bath. A dressing room was created that maintains the original Georgian molding. The entire apartment reflects a careful respect both for classical architecture and for eclectic English and Continental art and antiques.

Referring to the Yves Klein coffee table, Netto says: "Klein's estate makes a few of them each year. Two men wearing biohazard suits installed it. I'll never move it!"

Can an apartment change a life?

David Netto might say so. "It was my first 'serious' apartment. I was single and I guess it may have made me more attractive," he explains playfully, referring to his bicoastal romance with a California-based actress Ione Skye. "It certainly made me grow up faster. I had a kid within a year."

"I love Washington Square, especially the fact that it's about to be reborn. It's one of New York's real piazzas, small, busy and diverse. It is just funky enough, not a zoo like St. Mark's Place, where I first lived after college."

Looking for an apartment, Netto suspected something special was hidden beneath an unfortunate 80s renovation that had been inflicted on a 1924 building by Deutsch and Schneider: a miniature Park Avenue Georgian overlooking Washington Square. "It was a mess! But I was ready for a gut job, and eager to restructure the apartment.

After earning an masters degree in Architectural History at Columbia, dropping out of Harvard's architecture program, and recently opening his own design practice, Netto is hardly a novice at renovation. Known for the youthful spin he put on his friends' traditional apartments, he set out to do the same for himself.

He created room-to-room views by eliminating windowless inner corridors, dividing open spaces by playing with shades of white. "For the original Georgian-style exterior shell I used matte white. For the new architecture, where I removed the heart of the old plan, I used high gloss white lacquer."

Old Master drawings cover one sitting room wall. "On permanent loan from my father," he jokes. "After my mother died, I started a little modern art collection,"

OPPOSITE, LEFT *and* BELOW: *Opening up diagonal views from the center of the apartment to windows on the square was an important part of the architectural renovation.*

BELOW: *Making such a strong connection between the kitchen and dining room gave the kitchen a role as a front room, as if it were also on the park.*

pointing to a Twombly chalkboard on paper and an Yves Klein coffee table, embedded with blue pigment.

Two side tables from the 1939 World's Fair French Maritime Pavilion add gravitas, one supporting a Giacommetti-like lamp. A French neo-classical engraving from 1768 by Jean-Charles Delafosse sits on a late eighteenth-century Swedish architect's table. Nearby rests a console table whose design was inspired by the engraving, "L'Amérique," of which Netto owns a copy of the folio.

His dining room mixes a Basquiat painting, a whimsical model of a boat—which inspires a great deal of curiosity from guests—and a round 1840s Anglo-Irish dining table bought from Niall Smith, surrounded by Paul Kjaerholm Danish leather-upholstered chairs from the fifties. Guests look straight from the dining room into the kitchen, where a Charles X chandelier dangles daintily from a coral taffeta sleeve, over a simple wooden table and chairs by Alvar Aalto in front of a sleek Wolf range.

The sitting room acts as a buffer between the two bedrooms, and an intimate retreat from the white entertaining spaces. An Adnet lamp sits on an eighteenth-century Swedish drop-front secretary.

Mixing luxury with the unexpected in order to create a contemporary version of an elegant suite on the Normandie, he padded panels with geometric menswear fabric, added Zebra-wood doors, framed a plasma television screen as a painting, and draped jute and cow-skin rugs on the floor. "Very Halston, don't you think?" he asks, noting a mirrored column masking a gas main.

Netto's playful juxtapositions continue in his daughter Kate's room, which blends an Arp owned by Louise Nevelson, and a French dresser from the thirties—the latter inspired a piece in Netto Collection, his new line of children's furniture. A decorative frieze hides air-conditioning vents, running the entire length of the wall. "It looks less nervous, like a cornice," he explains.

Netto's own bedroom boasts nineteenth-century Zuber wallpaper panels, a Louis XVI desk chair from the Château de Groussay, a reproduction of a Georgian console table, and a Ralph Lauren bed. In order to make the room seem larger, Netto tried to evoke a panoramic view of Washington Square Park, using nineteenth-century wallpaper depicting outdoor scenes. "It's like a park within a park." Visitors, enchanted by such ingenuity, want to hire him on sight.

ABOVE: *Netto is fascinated by mechanical furniture, such as this English Regency adjustable table in his bedroom.*
LEFT: *Reflected in the master bath mirror is a small sculpture by Moholy-Nagy.*

On two floors of a limestone townhouse

built in 1903, lives Joan Rivers. It is one of a few remaining limestone townhouses designed by famed Philadelphia architect, Horace Trumbauer. Exiting a small, rickety, manually-operated elevator, one is hardly prepared for the architectural grandeur of the apartment she calls home.

Adjacent to the "ballroom" is a cozy study with pale-paneled walls, comfortable sofas, and a roaring fire. A terrace extends alongside the room, covered in roses by May.

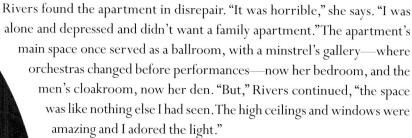

LEFT *and* OPPOSITE: *In the apartment's enormous central space— the former ballroom boasting twenty-three foot ceilings—the owner built columns and laid parquet floors. A Russian gilder painstakingly and artfully restored original boiseries. An antique Coromandel screen is used to divide the room, creating a separate sitting area.*
BELOW: *Eighteenth-century commodes that belonged to Rivers' mother flank a banquette below the gallery.*

Rivers found the apartment in disrepair. "It was horrible," she says. "I was alone and depressed and didn't want a family apartment." The apartment's main space once served as a ballroom, with a minstrel's gallery—where orchestras changed before performances—now her bedroom, and the men's cloakroom, now her den. "But," Rivers continued, "the space was like nothing else I had seen. The high ceilings and windows were amazing and I adored the light."

Rivers commissioned Louis Malkin, who had designed her California home, and architect Henry Stolzman to restore the original beauty. One of the challenges in the renovation was to incorporate not only her own furniture, but also that of her mother and mother-in-law, who had just died.

"I started collecting Fabergé in 1968 and wanted to display my pieces, along with my paintings. Wherever I go, they go, along with my mother's Russian chair and the Queen Anne globe from my late husband's family."

Rivers hosts grand parties in this palatial space, welcoming as many as fifty guests with piano music or a string quartet. For more intimate dinners, she uses a separate dining room. Evoking a candlelit jewel box, this dining room features ornate panels—originally from an eighteenth-century chateau—that once adorned the walls of the Astor Theatre's ladies room.

Hung in a central location is Van Dongen's powerful painting of his daughter writing a note, entitled "Milles Baisers." Nearby, a Russian table and chair sit among French and Continental furniture the owner has collected over many years. A Scottish clock plays music on the hour.

FOLLOWING PAGES: The dining room was redecorated four years ago by John Christensen. The ornate panels were originally in an eighteenth century chateau from where they were taken and hung in the ladies room in the old Astor Theatre. When the theatre was demolished, they went to auction where Rivers bought them and installed them in the apartment fifteen years ago.

OPPOSITE: *The bathroom space "epitomizes New York living—a series of compromises between function and comfort" as Rivers says. At left, her favorite thing, her easel.*
BELOW: *The bedroom is Rivers' favorite room—her sanctuary. On the night table is a Lalique vase that her mother bought on her honeymoon.*

A stairway was installed and lined with books. It leads up to Rivers' private quarters. Her bedroom is delicate, with a pastel palette. Pillows lushly cover the bed, from which the owner has a majestic view of the city. She keeps an easel in her marble bathroom, and often comes here to paint.

The owner did encounter one unusual obstacle, though, in creating her ideal home—ghosts! After purchasing the space, she observed peculiar phenomena, such as unexplained changes in the apartment's temperature. Parapsychologists from New York University were called in to assess the situation. Finally, the owner summoned a "ghostbuster" from New Orleans, who rid the townhouse of the ghosts of its former occupants. The renovations, of course, barely missed a beat.

High ceilings, a sweeping staircase,

OPPOSITE:

A classic William Harnett, "Still Life with Mug, Pipe, and New York Herald" from 1879 and an American neoclassical center table circa 1815 set the tone for the gracious entry foyer.

ABOVE: *American watercolors and drawings line the stairwell, including works by Edward Hopper and Reginald Marsh. These stairwell walls are hand-painted, and stenciled in tones of soft ochre and burnished gold.*

and the feeling of a private house excited Ellie Cullman and her husband, Edgar, who bought this thirteen-room Park Avenue duplex in 1985. The couple could see past the dreary battle-ship grey pallor to the gracious proportions and original moldings of this 1929 Rosario Candela apartment which was still occupied by its original tenants.

ABOVE: *Flanking a neo-classical Dutch chest in the front hall are four 1815 China trade paintings, which serve to remind the couple of their past travel to Canton harbor.*

In the living room, Tang dynasty horses and riders sit below a Francoise Gilot still life from the 1950s.

Undaunted, Cullman tackled the enormous job, using the apartment as a laboratory for her budding design practice. The duplex's classic Georgian-style architecture dictated a traditional late-eighteenth-century design vocabulary. She viewed the project more as a restoration than a renovation, and was committed to preserve the apartment's traditional details. When she centered and enlarged the doorway between the living and dining room she found a plaster artisan to replicate the living room's dental molding as well as to recast the library's acanthus leaf crown moldings. She was careful to re-border the parquet floors when moving walls.

The living room most dramatically demonstrates Cullman's love affair with English and American furniture, American paintings, and Asian antiques. Cullman studied history and art history at Barnard, and spent two years in Tokyo before returning in the seventies to work at Japan House Gallery and at the Museum of American Folk Art. The room's décor was inspired by a beige Persian Bidjar carpet with French scrolls in the center, made for the late nineteenth-century European export market. "I didn't want anything to look new," she explains. A George III carved and gilded over-mantel mirror makes the room glow.

LEFT: *The apartment reflects Ellie Cullman's love of things both Asian and American. While in Japan, the couple were enchanted by a nine-foot screen, depicting a lovely view of Kyoto in the early 1700s; they never dreamed that their future apartment would hold it so perfectly.*

The dining room began as an homage to the Chinese Parlor at Winterthur. At Gracie, the couple found forty feet of antique eighteenth-century Chinese wallpaper, portraying a traditional village marriage scene. But they needed seventy-six feet, so Gracie sent artists to hand paint the rest. "No one can tell the difference," Cullman adds confidently. A George III dining table, a cut-crystal Georgian chandelier, a Regency bull's-eye mirror, an English Regency black-lacquered collector's cabinet, and sixteen Hepplewhite chairs rest upon a late nineteenth-century Sultanabad carpet. Ming Chinese porcelain and Tang dynasty pottery figures (not visible) reinforce the Asian theme.

ABOVE: *Favorite decanters—claret jugs, ship's decanters, magnums—from Edgar Cullman's extensive collection of wine accessories have pride of place in the dining room, where they are always used at gatherings of family and friends.*

The cozy library, with its claret colored
walls and peacock blue Tabriz carpet, is
hung with a wide variety of American
painting, ranging from a nineteenth-
century watercolor by Childe Hassam to a
twentieth-century Cubist portrait by
Theodore Roszak. A Delft garniture sits
atop the mantel along with a Regency
giltwood and ebony convex mirror with
snake motif.

The Chinoiserie-patterned fabric upstairs in the master bedroom illustrates one aspect of Cullman's repertoire. "It's a calm oasis, not too fussy—for my husband," she says. Pale green walls display images of dancers: watercolors by American artists including Robert Henri and Abraham Walkowitz, and photographs by Henri Cartier Bresson and Barbara Morgan.

ABOVE: *The bedroom's palette of celadon and white is reinforced by the decorative accessories chosen: eighteenth-century Staffordshire saltglaze dishes, nineteenth-century creamware baskets (not visible) and an extensive Art Deco dressing table made of bone, with applied brass "E"s, Ellie's initial.*

Cullman's private study, on the other hand, is wildly exuberant: its painted ceiling serves as an homage to Robert Adam's sherbet palette, scrolling designs, and floral motifs. "I like to look up when I'm exercising, and this kind of painting epitomizes my favorite decorative style." Green and white checked fabrics cover the walls, curtains, and window seat, complementing the comfortable sofa and overstuffed chair, which are upholstered in old-fashioned printed linen. Serving as the room's centerpiece is a green-lacquered English Regency partners' desk, where she spends many hours, conjuring her well-respected designs.

ABOVE: *In Ellie's study, layered lighting—with chandeliers, table lamps, sconces, and picture lights—reflects an important part of her signature style, providing a warm glow to all her interiors.*

In this midtown pied-à-terre

the rooms sparkle, befitting a bachelor who loves to entertain and lives in Manhattan only a few months of the year. With the help of designer Scott Snyder, this apartment's owner created a space reminiscent of a classic 30s movie set, where one might find Fred Astaire and Ginger Rogers dancing glamorously on moonlit ebony floors.

PREVIOUS PAGES: *The dining room sideboard is verre églomisé, or gilded mirror, covered with signs of the zodiac. These mottled mirrors reflect the candlelit table, its center often filled with silvered shells and a collection of English silver spoon-warmers. An alabaster chandelier and a Regency screen divide the dining area from the hall.*

ABOVE: *The guest room doubles as an office, outfitted with computer and audio-visual equipment.*

RIGHT: *The living room walls, delicately lacquered in layers of grey and beige, evoke starlight. Sensuously curving Deco furniture dances in the glow of candles. The room is anchored by comfortable upholstered sofas, slipper chairs, and dark floors. An early modernist table—described by the owner as "industrial and machine-turned"—sits in the center of the room, made its focal point with a vase of lilies or branches.*

The building, built in 1911, with one apartment per floor, had been stripped down to its girders and divided into many smaller units in 1958. "We found old photographs of the building showing that it preceded the Ritz Towers, but its original façade was covered in white brick to make it look more modern."

ABOVE AND OPPOSITE: *"The bedroom is my favorite place, especially at night, when the view down Park Avenue is dazzling. It's quite a change from palm trees and the ocean. The sound-proof windows shut out all the noise and the city lights create a moving ribbon. At Christmas, the night time view is particularly brilliant after the Park Avenue tree lighting. I always come to town at that time of year to enjoy the holiday season in the city"*

Having lived with English interiors and wanting something totally different, but not stark, Art Deco seemed appealing as a general design style. The owner was drawn to its clean lines, still classical but more modernist than the furniture he lives with the rest of the year, in Florida.

The owner found that New York inspired a taupe and gray palette. "I had always lived with color and printed fabrics, but this time I wanted cool elegance and solids as a backdrop for period pieces." To this end, he began an entirely new art collection. He found pieces in Dallas, Paris, Miami, and in many galleries in New York. The challenge of discovery was part of the fun.

In the apartment's pale grey-lacquered entry hall, a silver Art Deco bowl filled with white flowers and a glass Regency screen shimmer. The monochromatic glow is enhanced by a collection of contemporary art, with works on paper by Joel Shapiro, a construction by Sophi Vari in the hall, a Julian Lethbridge in the bedroom hall and Scott Olson monotypes hanging in the dining room.

The tranquil bedroom is covered in taupe linen panels, with a Jim Dine charcoal and pastel drawing of Calla lilies. It features mirrored screens that serve to draw one's eye to the view of Park Avenue. This subtle design detail enhances the feeling of looking out over an endless Manhattan landscape, from an urban retreat above.

Twenty-foot ceilings, a forty-foot room…"

"This is my dream house, my fantasy," says Georgette Mosbacher. "When I first walked into [the living room], I loved the challenge of its scale. The possibility of opening up three rooms to have political evenings. Working fires. I knew this was it: the light, the majestic view of the Metropolitan Museum, the original painted ceiling intact."

PREVIOUS PAGES *and* RIGHT : *Table tops are covered with memorabilia from the owner's fascinating and diverse travels and accomplishments: a silver box inscribed by the King and Queen of Spain, belt buckles from Operation Desert Storm embedded on a Tiffany box, crystal hearts, lapis and malachite animals, Limoges boxes from the Bush family and the President of Chile, souvenirs from the Republican convention, and awards from the March of Dimes.*
OPPOSITE : *The burnished-pumpkin colored dining room holds a pair of George III mahogany-carved cabinets, from the Linsky collection. A Louis XVI-style ormolu-mounted mahogany clock, a matching barometer decorated with ormolu laurel and acanthus leaves, and a neo-classical ormolu Russian cut-glass chandelier from 1780 complete the jewel box effect. Guests often gather around the dining room's round table for political debate.*

ABOVE: *A nineteenth-century Louis XVI style ormolu-mounted Japanese lacquer and amboyna commode, stamped Charles-Guillaume Winckelsen, sits across from the piano. The combination of French and Chinese influence is very unusual.*

When she purchased the apartment in 1990, though, it had been untouched for nearly seventy years—built by architects Warren and Wetmore in 1926—and needed major rewiring and restructuring. With the help of designer Peter Balsam, the project took two full years to complete.

Mosbacher, flame-haired CEO of a cosmetics company, sits cross-legged on a plush sofa in her palatial living room. She explains why, in 1988, Aaron Schickler—a Kennedy portraitist—insisted on drawing her in charcoal. "He was challenged by my red hair and wanted to do the opposite." The portrait, now hanging above her piano and flanked by Empire-style ormolu appliques, strikingly captures its subject's colorful personality, as does the apartment.

Mosbacher's goal was to create a perfect setting for entertaining. She transformed the ballroom into a magnificent living room with built-in bookcases as enormous as her vast windows overlooking Fifth Avenue. Between these windows, a pair of English Adam gilt wood girandole mirrors reflect light, while nineteenth-century Italian marble busts rest on the sills. An original battleship-gray mantel was faux-marbled, and an Asian screen placed along one wall.

Giant sets of Art Deco doors support painted panels from Roman baths, below which bronze nymphs recline. The original painted ceiling's warm coral and Mediterranean blue pattern is echoed in the hues of the floral rug below. "We tried restoring the ceiling, but if you touch it, it turns to dust." Original moldings also remain.

ABOVE: *Two large centurions, a pair of 4' 10" bronze figures of the Furietti Centaurs, after the antique, one depicting Hercules, guard the foyer.*

RIGHT: *The library, its painted ceiling depicting an ancient maritime map, boasts a carved mahogany octagonal partner's desk from 1860, floor-to-ceiling bookshelves, and a nineteenth-century Persian Serapi rug.*

LEFT: *An antique tall case clock stands at the end of the hallway. However, says Mosbacher, "My most precious thing is my dog, Eve."*

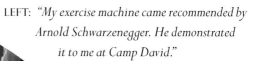

LEFT: *"My exercise machine came recommended by Arnold Schwarzenegger. He demonstrated it to me at Camp David."*

Mosbacher's private suite is the heart of the home, composed of three rooms. Who wouldn't envy an entire room devoted to evening gowns? A dressing room/beauty salon complete with plasma television and computer station? Imagine three rows of clothing racks, and glass shelves where handbags, sweaters, and shawls are coordinated in see-through cubbyholes.

BELOW: *"This is where I live!" explains Mosbacher. "It took me three years to get it (the room's sound system and Jacuzzi) right." A flat plasma screen television keeps her informed on world events and the market.*

LEFT: *In the guest bedroom chinoiserie and an antique kimono decorate the room.*

In contrast to this active space, the master bedroom is calm, with a crackling fireplace and painting flowers forming garlands on the ceiling. As the owner puts it: "Not bad for a girl who grew up modestly in Indiana and worked her way through college!"

This Gracie Square apartment

Around the room a column holds a 1919 Jo Davidson bust; there are works by Kenneth Noland, Horst and Tom Sachs, whose "Prada Happy Meal" and "Hermes Bag" rest on the piano.

was sold to Beth Rudin DeWoody in 1987 on Black Monday. "I lived around the corner and always loved this building!" she says. "The apartment was very simple, but I could see the beauty of its bones. It's a semi-duplex, with stairs that are not too steep!" With the help of architect Alan Wanzenberg and designer Jed Johnson, she took advantage of the duplex's dazzling view—stretching along the East River—and majestically high ceilings, adding classical details like columns and moldings.

PREVIOUS PAGES: *The hall—including the floor and central table—is literally stacked with art including work by Nan Goldin, Ed Ruscha, Andy Warhol, David Salle, and Kurt Schwitters. A trunk by fashion designer Jean-Paul Gaultier rests across from Gerrit Rietveld chairs and stone lions found in Palm Beach.*

LEFT *and* RIGHT: *The entire library has a Gothic theme, evoked by a guillotine cigar-cutter and Gothic clock and mantel, a Jean Dunand sculpture, a macabre Joel Peter Witkin photograph, and Heather Cox's skeleton made out of dollar bills.*

Her greatest challenge was to accommodate artfully vast collections gathered over the years at galleries, auctions, and flea markets and ranging from contemporary green glass to a Mexican chess set. DeWoody succeeded in filling every corner and covered every wall with a treasure trove of fascinating paintings, prints, photographs, furniture, ceramics and sculptures. She is passionate about artists ranging from Fornasetti to Joan Mitchell, to younger artists such as Jane South. She loves portraits, including one of her own mother painted in 1983 by Alex Katz, and a 1933 Virginia Beresford.

There is special meaning behind each piece she collects. "I bought a sculpture from the Chinese artist, Cai Guo-Qing, who created the fireworks for Central Park's centennial. He believes in Feng Shui and insisted on installing the artwork himself. It seems facing a hospital is bad luck, so he placed it in my window to guard my house!"

Off the hall is the library, which one enters through an enlarged and raised High Gothic door, by Wanzenberg. The library furniture includes a fifties table, a Viennese and an Adnet chair, and a Gio Ponti loveseat. Some of the objects have especially sentimental value for DeWoody: "The illuminated Egyptian alabaster urn belonged to my great friend, the late Robert Woolley of Sotheby's," she says.

The glittery grey dining room boasts a work by Sybil Andrews and an antique camera. Robert Lazzarini's multiple of a squashed, chipped cup sits regally on the sideboard, as does a silver Gorham tea set from 1907. Photographs of Marilyn Monroe by Bert Stern, Christopher Makos, Roxanne Lowit, and Gil Garfield adorn an entire wall.

ABOVE: Taking center stage, a John McLaughlin painting hangs over the fireplace
LEFT: A Jeff Koons chrome train set stretches down the center of the mirrored dining table, arriving ultimately at a silver model of heiress Barbara Hutton's house in Mexico.

OPPOSITE: *Expressly for the bathroom, Michele Oka Doner created a fanciful bronze vanity chair.*

BELOW: *The kitchen holds a cabinet of Rookwood pottery, as well as contemporary pieces the owner playfully calls "Breakfast Art": a piece of embroidery depicting Wonder Bread, and a dress composed of Sweet and Low packets.*

DeWoody's colorful, madcap bath and dressing room is covered in Pewabic tile, from a Detroit company associated with the 1800s Arts and Crafts movement. "They never stopped turning out tiles, but were only making pottery in the 80s. In 1986, I went to their factory and commissioned tiles based on their early work. It took several tries to get it right." This private area, a riot of bright and beautiful art—all illuminated by Tiffany lamps—epitomizes the apartment's overall design: fearless and fun, respecting the past and looking to the future.

Located in one of Manhattan's premier buildings,

the beauty of this apartment lies in its details, understated and subtle. Some apartments scream for attention, but not this one. Designed in 1929 by Rosario Candela, the apartment serves as an understated backdrop to an astonishing collection of ancient sculpture, fine art, and furniture, as well as personal mementos and flea market finds.

The owner had a clearly articulated philosophy for the apartment's design: "A reaction to the eighties chintz craze, nothing faux, no tassels. I didn't want people saying 'Oh my God, those taffeta curtains are unbelievable!' I wanted a calm neutral background that embraced my ancient sculpture. We were among the first to see the beauty of beige."

The sitting room, a symphony of beige, features a Picasso made of sand. A Viennese clock in the shape of a Polish cavalry officer, whose eyes move from side to side, chimes on the quarter hour. The clock sits on top of a long eighteenth-century English table between windows. Vying for the guests' attention are a sixteenth-century drawing by Passarotti, "The Two Demons," and a

sculpture of a head from the second century. "She's part of a colossus, a Roman copy from the Greek," the owner explains. Louis XVI French chairs covered in their original, colorful petit-point, Old Master drawings, and an ancient Egyptian bronze cat are also captivating. On the coffee table sits a bronze Greek arm, a gift from Bill Blass.

ABOVE: *In the peaceful library, one is greeted by a sculpture of a queen in the Egyptian style, from the time of Alexander the Great—three hundred B.C.E.—and a torso with original color from the same time period. A pair of Hubert Robert paintings represent the Pantheon and the Arch of Titus, ancient edifices that echo the library's classical theme. A painting by Vernet of a Spanish consul on a prancing white horse hangs above the settee.*

RIGHT: *A Joseph II desk from Vienna, where the couple had spent several years.*

In 1986, the apartment's fashionable owner decided to move from a majestic five-bedroom apartment—in the same building—to this smaller one, enlisting legendary designer Albert Hadley to oversee the transition. "I met Albert in 1970. We've worked on all my homes since then, bringing furniture along. I love his severe, restrained architectural style. It's a background for the things I collect, like my Degas bronze ballet dancer or a seventeenth-century bronze satyr. I knew the apartment well, friends owned it. I was ready for a change."

OPPOSITE: *Initially, two rooms adjoined the dining room. "Ridiculous!" said Hadley, who took down the wall and squared off its arch to match the opening in an adjacent living space. On either side of this new aperture, Hadley built yet more bookcases. Hadley's original creation, the morning room, is used for cozy dinners or intimate lunches overlooking the terrace.*

Originally part of a thirty-five room duplex, the new apartment occupied one floor, and its lower ceilings meant that some of the owner's favorite pieces had to go. "Do you want your mirrors sitting on the floor?" Hadley asked, encouraging her to discard and edit. The age of the apartment posed a challenge for the renovation. "We couldn't fix a

The dining room, lacquered a rich shade of chocolate brown, features green leather chairs surrounding a large, early nineteenth-century mahogany dining table. A mirrored screen, designed by Syrie Maugham, reflects the light from an outdoor terrace. "Famine" by Alexandre-Francois Desportes hangs over an eighteenth-century Italian inlaid side table, while Desportes's "Feast" hangs over a matching side table, on the opposite wall. A green-bordered Chamberlain Worcester porcelain service for twenty-two decorates the sideboard.

leak for years until we located the original canvas-rolled plans."

The owner was remarried to a renowned editor who came with a vast book collection. Because the apartment's former owners had used the apartment as a pied-a-terre—living in it only one month out of the year—the apartment had only one small bookcase. In order to build more, Hadley's suggested that the owner extend the wall over one library window.

Still pleased with Hadley's eighteen-year-old scheme, the lady of the house recently refreshed her sitting room, changing as little as possible, using the same fabrics. Why fight perfection? Assured and cultivated, this couple mixes the beauty of the past with the comfort of the present.

ABOVE: *A coral fan found by the owner on a on a dive in St. Barth's rests on a chest in the bedroom hall, as do a Hercules clock and paintings of a lost house, possibly by Humphrey Repton.*

OPPOSITE: *Hadley first opened up and then closed an original fireplace to better place the bed in the cheery master bedroom. Engravings of Egypt and Petra by David Roberts, dating to 1848, cover the walls. A nineteenth-century Russian desk and an Adam shield-back armchair sit below a Georgian mirror, bisque vases, and a Fulco di Verdura painting.*

Boasting fine views of the East River

this grand duplex is an extraordinary find. And although Marty Richards, the Oscar-winning owner, has assembled a museum-quality collection of art and furniture—including an ancient Roman statue of Poseidon, nineteenth-century lapis painted on glass, boiseries from an eighteenth-century French chateau, sconces from Versailles, and chairs from the Wrightsman collection—he does not take his treasures too seriously. A piano, played by friends like Steven Sondheim, Cy Coleman, Marvin Hamlisch, Julie Stein and Jerry Herman, means as much to him as any antique.

The library / den also holds the owner's trophys, among them his Best Picture Oscar, Golden Globe, and Tony Awards.

Builder James Stewart saw the potential of a forty thousand square foot property facing the East River and retained Willliam L. Bottomley of the architectural firm Bottomley, Wagner & White to develop a co-op, even as New York fell into the Great Depression. Completed in 1930, distinguished New Yorkers from Cornelius Vanderbilt Whitney on have lived here, enjoying some of the most luxurious apartments ever built.

Richards loves fine French furniture and gilding—he jokes that he was reincarnated from Versailles in the age of Louis XIV—while his late wife preferred English antiques, and paintings by American Impressionists. A great philanthropist, he has learned to put his riches in perspective. "From my wife, I learned that things are just things."

ABOVE: *Anthony Ingrao redesigned the apartment in shades of cream and pastels after the death of Richards' wife, but he kept her salon, which displays her silver collection along hand-painted walls.*

OPPOSITE: *In the dining room, Richards has hung "Oaxaca Market," by Millard Sheets. On the small table is a piece of Royal Copenhagen "Flora Danica" china.*

The master bath, created by Michael de Santis, is an exact copy of Napoleon's tent, painted on glass.

OPPOSITE, BELOW, *and* LEFT: *Ingrao followed his client's wishes, creating one of the most dramatic bedrooms in New York— complete with a Russian desk and silk-covered walls, using shades of gilded glass walls. Napoleon's letter ordering troops for Waterloo decorates the powder room.*

ABOVE: *The guest bedroom echoes the curtain swags although the effect is more comfort than grandeur.*

On a Tribeca street,

OPPOSITE: *Works by Korean potter Young-Jae Lee. On the wall hangs a ceramic Teatrino sculpture by Italian artist Fausto Melotti. In the forground sits a molded plywood chair by Scandinavian designer Grete Jalk.*

RIGHT: *Wilson's study. The desk ensemble was designed by Donald Judd.*

after ducking between trucks, one enters an industrial-looking building, climbs several flights of stairs in near darkness, and waits for the door to open, never expecting the surprise inside. Robert Wilson, avant garde director and artist—and trained architect—has created a unique, breathtaking space, part loft and part artistic laboratory.

The entry area contains Wilson's workspace, where plans and drawings are often spread out on a large round unique Aalto table. To the side of the table stands a rare large open-topped Chinese Neolithic urn. In the bottom corner is a flower-filled Lucite chair by Shiro Kuramata titled "Miss Blanche Chair" based on the character Blanche from Tennessee Williams' A Streetcar Named Desire.

For Wilson, art is life. Over the years, he has collected six thousand objects, dating from the prehistoric to the present. Here they are placed in carefully modulated clusters dictated by complex similarities or oppositions. Touring the loft, Wilson shares his understanding of each piece: an Eames child's chair, African spoons, Marlene Dietrich's shoes, an eighteenth-century stone from the top of a grave, a Marcel Breuer chair, a Sumbanese stone double-headed horse from a king's tomb, carved with Indonesian zoomorphic imagery. Other notable objects include turtles with carved monkeys from the Mentawi Islands off the coast of mainland Sumatra, prehistoric pottery shards, works of Danish potter Bodil Manz, and drawings by Fausto Melotti.

OPPOSITE: *Wilson's bedroom holds photographs of Gertrude Stein, Jack Smith, Merce Cunningham ballerina Sylvie Guillem's foot en pointe, Indonesian masks and Neolithic Chinese ceramics, photos by Man Ray and Cecil Beaton, a poster of Marlene Dietrich, a 256 AD Chinese torso, and a Donald Judd brass chair.*

In this space, the aesthetic of juxtaposition determines design rather than period or provenance. Richard Serra's rusted steel model for "New York" sits beside a Bauhaus child's chair, and primitive artifacts. Photographs occupy an entire wall, including portraits of William Burroughs, Bette Davis, and Albert Einstein, while another is covered with shields, carved monkey panels from pre-Darwin Indonesia, and doors from Kalimantan. Wilson's own drawings rest above 1950s Gio Ponti chairs, including the black and white "Superleggera," the model number "669"—which is light enough to be lifted by a child with one finger—and the serpentine "969." An original chair by Wilson enti-

ABOVE: *What is now the bathroom was once the artist John Chamberlain's spray-painting room. The paint was left untouched by Wilson.*

tled "Never Doubt I Love," based on Hamlet's letter to Ophelia, shares space with chairs by Frank Lloyd Wright, Alvar Aalto, Gerrit Rietveld, and Gerald Summers.

LEFT: *Wilson began collecting when he was seven, asking his uncle for a chair. His lifelong interest led to the creation of his first chair design, which hangs in a corner of his loft. The 1969 wire-and-mesh chair, made for "The Life and Times of Sigmund Freud," still intrigues Wilson. "When lit properly, its image between shadow and light exactly replicates the chair," he explains, noting the chair's mirror image on the wall. To the right of the chair is a large glass sculpture of Stanislav Libensky, a 1950s Czech painter and sculptor, and works by his students, which Wilson began collecting.*

OPPOSITE: *Sun streams through into the loft, reflecting the Hudson River through giant exposed windows.*

ABOVE : *A Carlo Molino door serves as the backdrop to the three Amadeus Chairs, created by Wilson in 1991, that resemble twigs. The chairs were carried on the heads of priests in Wilson's production of Mozart's "The Magic Flute" for the Paris Opera.*

LEFT : *Formal rows divide and define the dizzying array that sits, hangs and lines the two main rooms.*

Wilson is also drawn to peaceable kingdoms. Shaker tables, rockers and children's chairs appeal to his artistic vision. "Simplicity of design in a utopian community speaks to me. Central to their philosophy is the idea that heaven could be created on earth. An 1836 Shaker chair can balance on its back legs, ethereal and light."

The owner of this apartment has performed his own aesthetic balancing act: blending fantastic objects from many periods into one ordered, harmonious universe.

Acknowledgments

I owe many thanks to John Mashek, President of the Preservation Foundation of Palm Beach, who introduced me to Jamee Gregory after I had the pleasure of producing a book for the Foundation. To Charles Miers, Publisher at Rizzoli, and to David Morton and Douglas Curran, whose comments and advice were always welcome. To Jennifer Tarr, who kindly undertook the editing, and then Rachel Altfest. To my wife, Yoko Nomura, and my three children, Taira, Mia, and Kei, who bore with me some long hours and occasionally shared in the excitement.

This book has been made a pleasure to produce through the cooperation of so many parties and their willingness to accommodate the needs of our team. Backstage as well, we had unstinting help and many cups of tea. We cannot name you all but you know we are enormously grateful.

—C.D.

I would like to thank my friends, whose apartments are featured in this book, for their patience and trust. My husband Peter, my daughter Samantha, my sister Michele, and my parents Arlene and Sherman Tucker stood by me and always offered support. I am grateful to John Mashek for introducing me to Charles Davey and to Marshall Heyman, Hugh Freund, and Stanislas de Quercize for giving me the courage to write my first book.

—J.G.

Photo Credits

All photographs are © the photographers.

All the photographs are by Mick Hales with the following exceptions:
Tina Wipfler pp 120-127
Charles Davey pp 77bl, 82bl, 84bl, 102tr, 133bl, 136t&b, 139r, 205tr, 207tr

First published in the United States of America in 2004 by
RIZZOLI INTERNATIONAL PUBLICATIONS, INC.
300 Park Avenue South, New York, NY 10010
www.rizzoliusa.com

ISBN: 0-8478-2663-5
LCCN: 2004094406

© 2004 Rizzoli International Publications, Inc.
Photographs © 2004 Mick Hales, Tina Wipfler, Charles Davey
Text © 2004 Jamee Gregory

Front cover: See page 46. Photograph by Mick Hales
Back cover: See page 83. photograph by Mick Hales

Charles Davey LLC Book Productions
Concept, art direction, design, production and manufacturing by Charles Davey LLC
Edited by Jennifer Tarr and Rachel Altfest

Printed and bound in China

2004 2005 2006 2007 2008 / 10 9 8 7 6 5 4 3 2 1